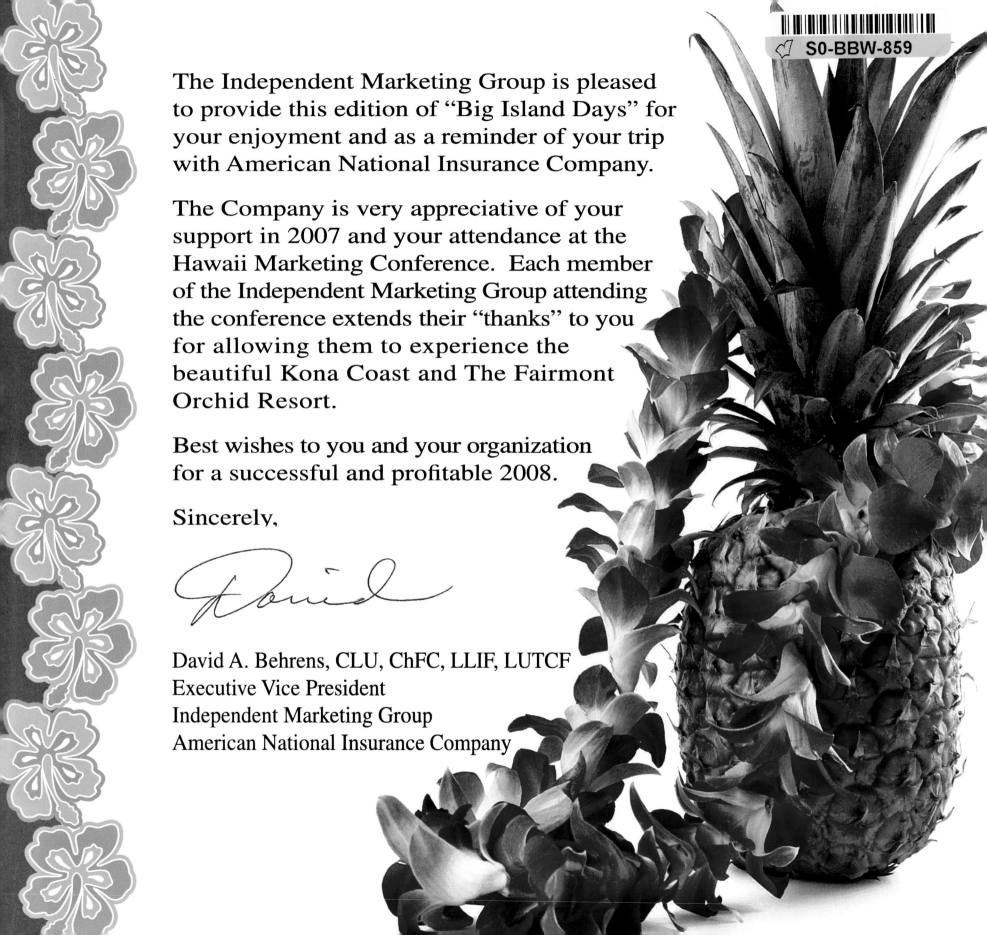

The Independent Marketing Group is pleased to provide this edition of "Big Island Days" for your enjoyment and as a reminder of your trip with American National Insurance Company.

The Company is very appreciative of your support in 2007 and your attendance at the Hawaii Marketing Conference. Each member of the Independent Marketing Group attending the conference extends their "thanks" to you for allowing them to experience the beautiful Kona Coast and The Fairmont Orchid Resort.

Best wishes to you and your organization for a successful and profitable 2008.

Sincerely,

David A. Behrens, CLU, ChFC, LLIF, LUTCF
Executive Vice President
Independent Marketing Group
American National Insurance Company

BIG ISLAND DAYS

Secluded quiet beach parks dot the Big Island's coast line. Kēōkea Beach Park in North Kohala, pictured here, offers grassy lawns and a picnic pavilion. It is favored by local fishermen.

BIG ISLAND DAYS

PHOTOGRAPHY BY KIRK LEE AEDER
TEXT BY SOPHIA V. SCHWEITZER

HAWAIIAN DAYS

ISBN 1-56647-735-2
Library of Congress Catalog Card Number:
2005928617
Design by Emily R. Lee

First Printing, October 2005
1 2 3 4 5 6 7 8 9

HAWAIIAN DAYS
1215 Center Street, Suite 210
Honolulu, Hawai'i 96816
Ph: 808-732-1709 / Fax: 808-734-4094
Email: mutual@mutualpublishing.com
www.mutualpublishing.com

Printed in Korea

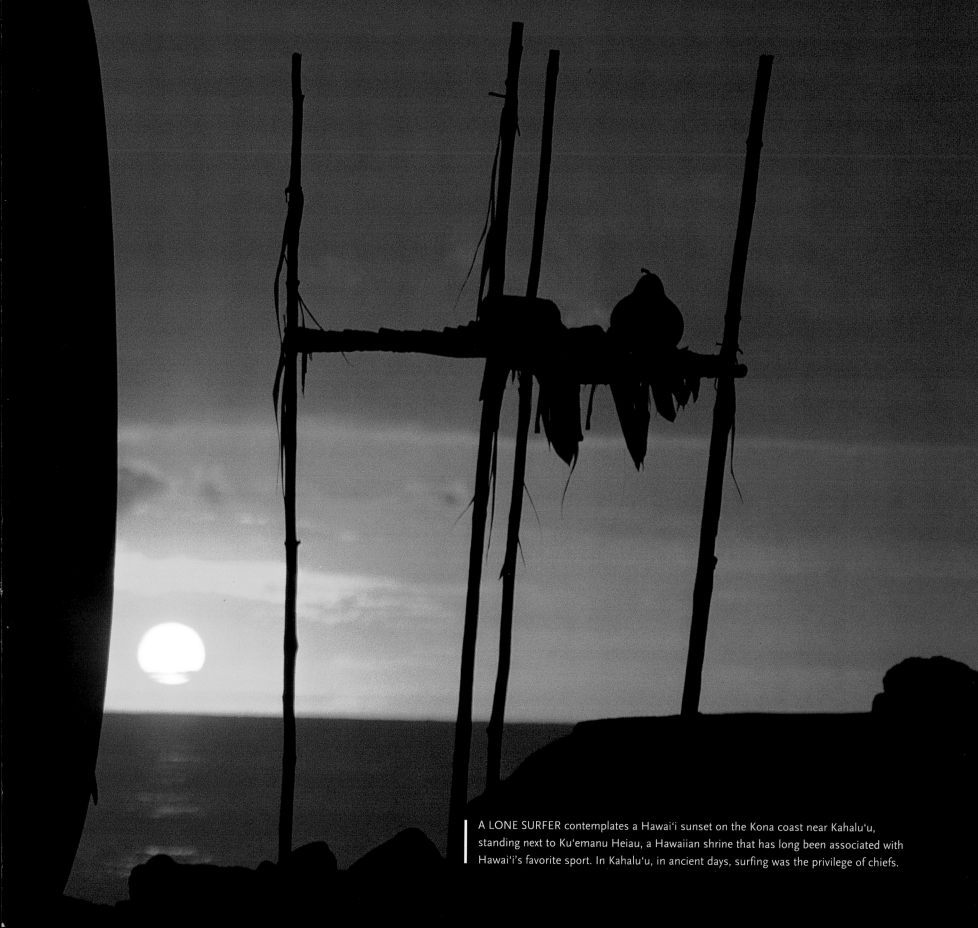

A LONE SURFER contemplates a Hawai'i sunset on the Kona coast near Kahalu'u, standing next to Ku'emanu Heiau, a Hawaiian shrine that has long been associated with Hawai'i's favorite sport. In Kahalu'u, in ancient days, surfing was the privilege of chiefs.

On the Big Island, the Hawaiian arts and traditions are vibrantly alive, agriculture keeps volcanic slopes green, windsurfers brave the waves, and tropical gardens abound.

TABLE OF CONTENTS

INTRODUCTION

The largest island in the Hawaiian archipelago, twice the size of all the other islands combined, the Big Island offers a kaleidoscope of historical, cultural, and natural beauty. Diverse and varied, this is a land of waterfalls, misty forests, black-sand beaches, snow-covered summits, and glowing lava, a land of fire and ice. Six districts, which fell in place in early times, each captures a different aspect of the Big Island's truths.

Around 300 AD, the first Hawaiian settlers may have arrived in the district of Ka'ū. Around the island, ruins of majestic temples still tell the story of powerful chiefs and priests. The Hawaiians planted taro, their staff of life. In Hāmākua's Waipi'o Valley, taro continues to thrive.

King Kamehameha was born on the Big Island, in the district of Kohala. In 1810, this great warrior achieved his goal of uniting the islands under one rule. The colors of royalty are still vibrantly alive, especially during ceremonies on King Kamehameha Day.

Kohala's rolling pasture lands trace their origins to wild cattle, introduced in the late 1700s, and domesticated by the Big Island ranches. Rodeos celebrate the tradition of Spanish-Hawaiian cowboys, paniolo, masters of the slack key guitar and the lariat.

In 1779, the British explorer Captain James Cook sailed into Kealakekua Bay in Kona, and irrevocable changes began. The Hawaiian religion collapsed under the weight of western values. In 1820, the first missionaries from Boston set foot on land in Kona. Hawaiian arts and traditions—including the sacred hula dance—would go underground. Structures built in the 1800s bear witness to these tumultuous times.

Sugar plantations would dominate the Big Island's landscape by the late 1800s. Thousands of immigrant laborers arrived. In a multiethnic melting pot, they added their cultural traditions to Hawaiian history. Little sugar towns dot the countryside from Hāmākua to Ka'ū.

One of the Big Island's many windward waterfalls, the cascading Kapoloa Falls in North Kohala drops over a narrow ditch trail that was carved into a 1,000-foot cliff in 1905. On private property, the site is accessible by permission only.

In the mid-1900s, tourism picked up. These days, sport fishing and endurance competitions attract thousands. Splendid golf courses sprawl along the Kona and Kohala coasts. Hawaiian activities such as paddling and surfing have been revived. A tradition of coffee farming has taken hold in Kona. Hilo is home to the state's largest hula festival.

Over all these changes tower the Big Island's volcanoes. On the flanks of 13,677-foot Mauna Loa fumes Kīlauea, possibly the most active volcano on earth. Its glowing lava has flowed without interruption since 1983 and has dramatically altered Puna's shores. This book, *Big Island Days*, ends with photographs of the highest mountain peak in the Pacific, 13,796-foot Mauna Kea, which reaches into the clearest of skies. Mauna Kea's summit is a sacred Hawaiian site, a gateway to the universe. Here, ancient traditions, unparalleled natural beauty, extreme conditions, and modern science converge. This is the Big Island.

Far Right: At Lapakahi State Historical Park in the district of Kohala, ruins of an ancient Hawaiian fishing settlement have been partially restored. Lapakahi's calm waters belong to a Marine Preserve.

HILO

Trade winds rise and clouds release abundant rain in the district of Hilo, which bridges the saddle between Mauna Kea and Mauna Loa on the Big Island's windward side. Hilo is a land of rainbows and rivers, of tropical gardens with orchids, anthuriums, and flowering trees. Its hidden beach coves open to a rough coastline ribboned by cascading waterfalls.

The town of Hilo hugs a sheltered bay, a favorite place for fishing and swimming. The surf can be great. The bay gives access to an off-shore islet with healing freshwater springs.

In Hawaiian times, powerful chiefs resided in Hilo. It became the site of the royal court. Queen Lili'uokalani spent many summer days in Hilo town, as did King Kalākaua, who revived Hawaiian music and dance. A garden was named in honor of the queen. Hilo's Merrie Monarch Festival, a celebration of the sacred hula dance and the Hawaiian arts, was named for the "merrie" King.

In the early 1800s, Sarah and David Lyman, missionaries from Boston, settled in, and built a frame house that has been preserved.

Sugar altered the quiet, sleepy bay front with plantation-style buildings in which, today, galleries and eateries thrive. But sugar was never Hilo's only crop. Its sprawling macadamia nut orchards contribute to a large sweet-crunchy industry, while colorful orchid gardens are plentiful.

Hilo town holds the county seat.

Named for Hawai'i's "Merrie Monarch," King Kalākaua, Hilo's world-famous Merrie Monarch Festival is a week-long celebration of the hula that draws dancers from around the world. Thousands watch the competitions, held annually after Easter Sunday.

Above: In the morning, when the sun falls just right, rainbows shimmer in the spray mists of Rainbow Falls, above downtown Hilo, and seem to drop into a deep, dark pool.

Far Right: Said to be the oldest frame building in the state, dating back to the mid-1800s, the Lyman Mission House and Museum shows a still life of missionary days. Missionaries David and Sarah Lyman were sent to Hilo in 1832 and would serve Hilo for more than fifty years.

Far Left: Passionate about surfing, Ben Jaquias shapes boards at his shop in Hilo when he is not riding the waves.

Surfers watch the waves in the early morning hours on the black sand of Honoli'i Beach Park, just north of Hilo. The waters here provide a prime surfing and boogie boarding spot.

Above: Along a scenic route north of Hilo and edging the cliffs of scenic Onomea Bay flourishes the jungle of the Hawai'i Tropical Botanical Garden. More than 2,000 species thrive in this 17-acre valley garden, which got its start in 1977.

Right: In a deep gorge in the Wailuku River, just above Hilo, the forces of erosion have left giant depressions known as "boiling pots." During heavy rains, river water rushes and roils to create a series of swirling pools and waterfalls.

Above: Macadamia nuts hide inside smooth, hard shells, encased by thick, green husks. It is said that up to 300 pounds per square inch of pressure may be required to remove the shells.

Left: The Mauna Loa Macadamia Nut Factory, about five miles south of Hilo, allows visitors a glimpse of its daily operations. Macadamia nuts are often sorted by size, and crushed pieces are removed to be used in baked goods such as mac nut pies.

Far Left: In the district of Hilo, hundreds of acres of well-tended orchards contribute to one of the islands' largest agricultural industries, the macadamia nut, first planted in 1879 as an ornamental.

Hugging a calm bay, the waterfront of Hilo town sprawls between two rivers, Wailoa and Wailuku. It features green gardens and peaceful ponds. Tsunamis in 1946 and 1960 destroyed the area twice, leading to the creation of a greenbelt buffer zone.

Above: A cultural tradition rooted in early Hawaiian history, canoe paddling has become a favorite team sport for islanders. Hilo Bay hosts major paddle events, such as the one shown here.

Right: Hawai'i's traditional canoe paddle is a handcrafted work of art. Skilled, dedicated woodworkers, themselves usually paddlers with intimate knowledge of the ocean, use a variety of techniques. In Hawaiian days, koa was a favored wood.

Above: On the Waiākea Peninsula, east of Hilo Bay, Japanese-style bridges and peaceful ponds accentuate the serene gardens of Lili'uokalani Park, named for Hawai'i's last queen.

Right: A modern, pedestrian bridge connects Hilo's Lili'uokalani Park to one of Hawai'i's oldest healing sites, Mokuola—its spring waters were said to have curative qualities. Better known as Coconut Island, the small park is a favorite fishing and picnic spot.

Left: The town of Hilo is home to about one third of the Big Island's 150,000 residents (Census 2000: 148,677). Its bay front was spruced up around the turn of the millennium. Renovated plantation-era buildings offering an eclectic array of galleries, restaurants, and shops.

Below: A young hula dancer adorned with flower leis awaits her turn.

First celebrated in 1963, the Merrie Monarch Festival seeks to perpetuate the traditional arts and culture of Hawai'i through the sacred hula dance. The kahiko-style of hula, shown here, taps into Hawai'i's ancient roots. Wearing traditional costumes, dancers chant the stories of their ancestors, while expressing reverence for the natural world.

Above: Hilo has been called "the orchid capital of the world," and the Hilo area produces almost half of all commercially grown tropical blooms in the state. South of Hilo, Akatsuka Orchid Gardens, pictured here, welcomes visitors.

Right: The pebbled Black Sand Beach of Honoli'i, a favorite spot for local surfers, cradles underneath Highway 19, the road that circles the island.

PUNA

At the most eastern tip of the Big Island, on the slopes of Mauna Loa and Kīlauea, the district of Puna is defined by fiery lava flows and volcanic steam. Molten magma from Kīlauea's most recent eruption, which started in 1983, has erased dozens of homes, a broad black-sand beach, and sacred Hawaiian sites. It has added new land. On the lava's unforgiving path, eerie lava sculptures have replaced rain forests of 'ōhi'a trees. Near the coast, the volcano's thermal energy heats springs.

Puna is home to a section of Hawai'i Volcanoes National Park. Dedicated to the rare native flora and fauna that inhabit a volcanic landscape, the park also monitors the volcano's lava flow. On the Park's higher elevations, the nēnē flies, the endangered Hawaiian goose that has adapted its webbed feet to Mauna Loa's lava fields.

The road from Hilo to Kīlauea Caldera traverses Puna's landscape. It passes orchid farms and macadamia nut orchards, as well as small sugar towns with rickety sidewalks and storefronts that recall the heyday of old.

Near Pāhoa, rescued from the lava, a small Catholic church commemorates two missionaries who surrendered themselves to the task of aiding suffering Hawaiians struck by Hansen's Disease. Narrow roads from Pāhoa lead east, where Puna hugs a rocky coastline and the fishing is good.

Above: Gnarly sculptures in Lava Tree State Park, off Highway. 132, are silent witnesses to Mauna Loa's powers of creation and destruction. When, in 1790, molten lava hit Puna's rain forest, it hardened around the 'ōhi'a trees to form lasting molds. The trees themselves quickly died.

Right: A finger of ropey, fluid pāhoehoe lava pulses forward on a journey of least resistance down Kīlauea's slopes. On the surface, the magma crusts over immediately. On the inside temperatures may reach 2,000 degrees.

Above: Puna's shoreline is a favorite fishing spot for local fishermen, who throw their nets to catch 'ōpelu (silver mackerel scad), āholehole (Hawaiian flagtail), and other small fish.

Left: Anchialine ponds of brackish water fringe the Puna coast line. Connected to the ocean, the ponds move with the tides, and attract native fish life and birds.

FATHER
DAMIEN DEVEUSTER

MOTHER
MARIANNE COPE

Above: Star of the Sea Painted Church, built in the 1930s, was rescued from encroaching lava flows in the early 1990s and moved to its present location above the Kalapana and Kaimū Coast.

Left: Stained-glass windows in Puna's Star of the Sea Painted Church depict two famous, beatified Catholic figures, Father Damien and Mother Marianne. They surrendered themselves to aiding Hawaiʻi's many victims of Hansen's disease, exiled to a colony on Molokaʻi. Father Damien began his missionary path in the islands in Puna in 1865.

Above: Once abundant, the endangered Hawaiian goose, nēnē, has fallen victim to hunters, rats, mongooses, dogs, and cats. Named State Bird of Hawai'i, it navigates Mauna Loa's rough lava with specially adapted, partially webbed feet.

Right: Hot, glowing lava plunges into the ocean at Kamoamoa, at the end of the Chain of Craters Road in Puna. The lava has traveled about six miles from Kīlauea's Pu'u 'Ō'ō vent. On brittle benches formed by hardened lava, which can easily collapse, a few brave visitors watch.

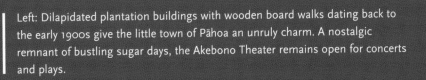

Left: Dilapidated plantation buildings with wooden board walks dating back to the early 1900s give the little town of Pāhoa an unruly charm. A nostalgic remnant of bustling sugar days, the Akebono Theater remains open for concerts and plays.

Above Right: As lava drops into the ocean, steam vapors hiss upward in a display of splash and spray. The mists are toxic, however. In an interplay of oxygen, water, and salt, the lava's sulfur dioxide reacts to form caustic fumes.

Above Left: At Ahalanui Park, volcanic steam heats a brackish pond. The water may not be safe for swimming, but tall coconut trees offer shaded views of Puna's rough Kapoho Coast.

Right: Kīlauea's lava flows have destroyed parts of Puna even as new land is formed. In 1990, lava swallowed the old fishing town of Kalapana and the famous black-sand beach of Kaimū. Beyond the lava, however, a new beach formed, where young coconuts are trying to sprout.

Below: A woman practices a sacred hula dance, wearing a hand-woven, traditional costume.

Above: Plumes of volcanic steam rise from Puna's coastline as molten, fiery magma from Puʻu ʻŌʻō vent flows into the ocean. Drifting rain squalls and a rough ocean surf augment Kīlauea's display of volcanic magnificence.

Right: Molten, glowing pĀhoehoe lava ripples underneath a hardening crust. Briefly visible through sudden openings, it gives the rough landscape a surreal, eery, and ever-changing glow.

Above: Built in 1941, Hawai'i Volcanoes National Park's historic hotel Volcano House traces its origins to the earliest days of tourism in the Islands. In the current structure, fireplace embers allegedly have been kept alive since 1877. In 1866, Mark Twain was a Volcano House guest.

Left: Lava from Kīlauea Volcano in the early 1990s destroyed villages and homes, but circled around Waha'ula Heiau, built in the 1300s. In 1997, however, molten lava swallowed the temple.

Ropey, smooth, and shimmering, pāhoehoe lava oozes forth from Kīlauea's East Rift Zone. Surging forth from the hottest magma in the world, the lava pushes downhill. While a crust forms as soon as lava is cooled by the air, lava underneath the surface continues its journey and occasionally pops through, as if in search of a new path.

Above: A glimpse inside Thurston Lava Tube at Hawai'i Volcanoes National Park shows how lava travels through a tube that was formed by an outer crust. The lava tube is an estimated 400 years old.

Left: Kīlauea Volcano has been continuously active since 1983, when lava started erupting from its Pu'u 'Ō'ō vent on the East Rift Zone, shown here. Craters form when magma drains out.

Above: Lava does not pay attention to rights-of-way. It has blocked numerous island routes including the famous Chain of Craters Road.

Left: The Devastation Trail in Hawai'i Volcanoes National Park leads through a barren landscape. In 1959, cinders and ashes from Kīlauea Iki covered this area's rain forest of tree ferns and 'ōhi'a trees. The forest is slowly recovering.

KAʻŪ

The plains of the vast district known as Kaʻū run from the summits of Mauna Loa and Kīlauea down to the Big Island's most southern point. It is said that here, at Ka Lae, the first Hawaiian settlers moored. They found in the deep ocean waters off Kaʻū's shores rich fishing grounds. Historical reminders remain.

At South Point, the winds are so fierce and continuous that engineers generate electricity through rows of humming mills. It is home to a rare green-sand beach, formed when Mauna Loa erupted with semiprecious olivine in its magma.

A broad expanse of a genuine black-sand beach embraces the coastline farther east, at Punaluʻu, where the reefs attract green sea turtles, and groves of swaying palm trees provide shade from the sun.

Sugar in Kaʻū phased out in the 1990s. Kaʻū's small sugar towns are opening bakeries, coffee shops, and fruit-and-flower stands that celebrate its agricultural heritage.

Most of Hawaiʻi Volcanoes National Park lies in Kaʻū. At its center stands the old Volcano House, or, at least, the 1941 version of a hotel deeply rooted in the Island's tourism industry. Founded in 1916, Hawaiʻi Volcanoes National Park continues to expand to protect the Big Island's most remote district, Kaʻū.

Above: In summertime, sweet, crisp starfruit (carambola) can be found on roadside fruit stands.

Right: Just east of South Point, a hiking trail leads to remote Green Sand Beach, where the ocean is dangerous but the sand is rich. Semiprecious olivine, deposited during Mauna Loa's volcanic eruptions, gives the beach its sparkle.

Above: A National Historic Landmark, South Point, or Ka Lae in the Hawaiian language, may have been the place where the first Polynesians to settle the Hawaiian islands arrived, perhaps as long as 1,700 years ago. Fishermen erected shrines here to honor the area's rich fishing grounds.

Left: Cliffside ladders near South Point, Hawai'i's most southern tip, provide access to dangerous swimming waters, which does not stop local youth. Fishermen string ropes to the rocks to reach the area's rich fishing grounds.

Left: Green Sea Turtles are protected by the United States Endangered Species Act.

Far Left: Green Sea Turtles frequent Punaluʻu's black sand beach, favoring its shallow reefs and cold oceanic waters fed by springs.

Only the most talented windsurfers—and those with high levels of risk tolerance—dare to challenge the choppy, stormy waters that prevail around the South Point area of Ka'ū.

Right: Secluded black-sand beaches, fringed by coconut palm groves, hug the coast-line of Kaʻū.

Far Right: On the windswept, grassy plains of South Point, the windmills of Kamāʻoa Wind Farm fill the air with an eerie sound.

Punaluʻu Beach Park in South Kaʻū is one of the most accessible black-sand beaches on the island. Its coconut groves, ponds, and exposed reefs make it a favorite tourist spot. Its black sand was formed when lava met the ocean and exploded. Wave erosion further polished the sand.

KONA

Spanning the leeward, western slopes of Mauna Loa and Hualālai, the district of Kona has been shaped by all the great forces that have swept through island history. Long before westerners arrived, this was a place of royalty. Its Place of Refuge—a national park—bears silent witness to a time of great chiefs and their priests.

At Kealakekua Bay, in 1779, the British explorer Captain James Cook anchored his ships. Cook was killed in unfortunate misunderstandings. His visit would lead to irrevocable change.

In 1820, Boston missionaries set foot on Kona land. A church built in 1837 survives. Hawaiian culture with its fine crafts and deeply spiritual beliefs would go underground, but a palace built in 1838 tells of royal times.

Coffee came to Kona in the 1820s. A labor-intensive product, it struggled for over 150 years until, in the 1990s, it finally emerged as a gourmet crop.

Kailua-Kona became serious about tourism in the late 1950s. A renewed celebration of surfing and paddling, sacred activities in Hawaiian times, would carry over to modern sports events that now draw athletes from around the world. Game-fishing tournaments and endurance competitions such as Kona's famous Ironman Triathlon attract thousands. Kailua-Kona, at the center of one of the state's most historic districts, is today also one of the state's most active seaside towns.

Above: Come late summer, a profusion of coffee cherries weighs down trees in Kona's coffee belt.

Right: The calm waters and white sands of Hōnaunau Bay in South Kona served as a royal canoe landing in early Hawaiian days. This was the site of Puʻuhonua o Hōnaunau, the sacred Place of Refuge, where commoners and warriors could find safety from harm.

Above: Big-game fishing has become one of Kona's greatest tourist attractions. Each August, hundreds of anglers flock to the district for Kona's Billfishing Tournament.

Left: In the shelter of Hualālai Volcano, Kailua-Kona has transformed itself from a sleepy fishing village into a bustling seaside town, yet has preserved its history. This photograph shows Moku'aikaua Church, the oldest surviving Christian church in the islands, built in 1837.

Above: Endangered and protected by federal and state laws, the Hawaiian monk seal lives mostly near the northwestern Hawaiian islands, but can occasionally be found sunning itself on a Big Island beach. It is thought that less than 1,500 of these animals exist today.

Right: White Sands Beach Park, south of downtown Kailua-Kona, is also known as "Magic Sands." When high surf rolls in, the sand retreats offshore and temporarily disappears. This popular little cove is great for snorkeling and boogie boarding.

Above: Built in 1838 by Governor Kuakini, Huliheʻe Palace once was a favorite summer residence for royalty. Restored by the Daughters of Hawaiʻi, the palace has reopened as a museum.

Left: The royal coat of arms of the Kingdom of Hawaiʻi, also the seal of the state, marks the entrance of the royal Huliheʻe Palace with the motto ua mau ke ea o ka aina i ka pono—the life of the land is perpetuated in righteousness.

Far Left: Vivid Bible scenes and whimsical patterns on the walls, columns, and ceiling of the Roman-Catholic church St. Benedict in Hōnaunau, built in 1896, earned it the name "Painted Church."

Above Left: When cloud covers settle over South Kona in the late afternoon, rainbows often accentuate the serenity of the Place of Refuge, Puʻuhonua o Hōnaunau.

Above Right: Crimson sunsets belong to the Kona Coast. The smoldering orange colors are sometimes deepened by the presence of vog, the volcanic mists that drift over from Kīlauea Volcano.

Right: A rare replica of a traditional Hawaiian outrigger canoe sails off the Kona Coast at sunset. In its construction, only koa and other woods indigenous to the islands were used.

Left: A team of paddlers takes off from Kamakahonu, in the calm waters of Kailua Bay. Moku'aikaua Church is in the background.

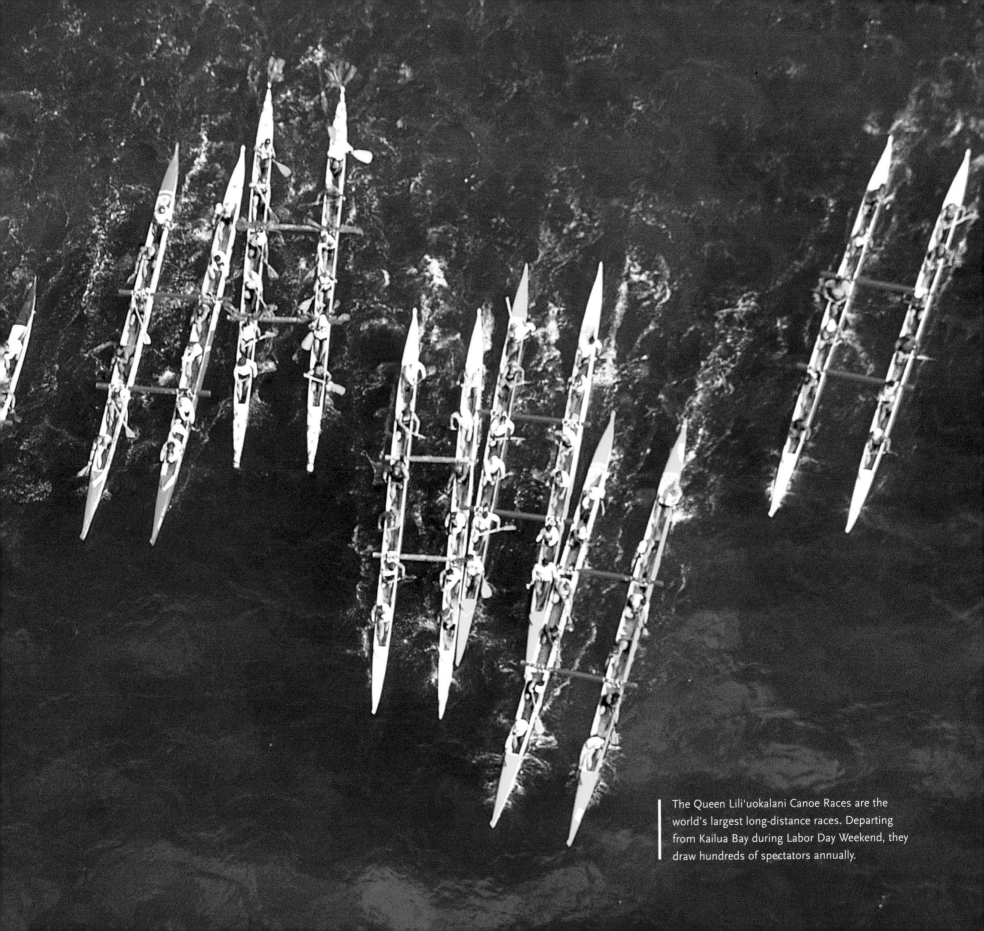

The Queen Liliʻuokalani Canoe Races are the world's largest long-distance races. Departing from Kailua Bay during Labor Day Weekend, they draw hundreds of spectators annually.

Above: The famous Kona Coffee Belt spans about 3,600 acres of orchards from Hōlualoa to Hōnaunau and finds a center in the coffee region surrounding Captain Cook, shown here. Coffee thrives on Kona's volcanic up-country slopes, where afternoon clouds provide cooling mists.

Right: On the oceanfront grounds of Hulihe'e Palace, hula dancers often gather to practice and perform.

Kona's annual Ironman Triathlon, the largest sporting event in Hawai'i, draws thousands of visitors eager to watch the ultimate endurance test. Athletes must finish a 2.4-mile swim, a 112-mile bike ride, and a 26.2-mile marathon.

Right: Peter Reid, multiple winner of the Kona Ironman, crosses the finish line.

TRIATHLON WORLD CHAMPION

8:22.35 TIMEX

Above: Waves crash over the stone seawall that borders Aliʻi Drive in Kailua-Kona—an excellent place to watch Kona's fishing boats angling in the area's rich fishing grounds.

Left: A young fisherman gathers his catch in the shallow waters of a tidepool in Keauhou, south of Kailua-Kona.

Above: Reconstructed, wooden temple images guard the thatched house known as Hale o Keawe, named for a chief who resided at Puʻuhonua o Hōnaunau in the 1700s. After Keawe's death, the hale became a mausoleum for his and other chiefs' bones, which increased the sacredness of the place.

Left: Tide pools teeming with marine life border Puʻuhonua o Hōnaunau. Within a massive L-shaped stone wall, still standing today, ancient Hawaiians in danger of their lives found refuge, safety, and a second chance. The Place of Refuge is a national park.

Above: Pro surfer Shane Dorian, born and reared in Kailua-Kona, rides a big Kona wave.

Right, inset: Dorian busts the air in waters off Kailua-Kona, proving that surfing ultimately is all about having fun.

Right: The Big Island draws top athletes to its big-wave surfing spots. With the sun setting over the Kona Coast, Japanese pro surfer Shuji Kasuya enjoys a few quiet moments on the shore.

Right: About eighteen miles south of Kailua-Kona, across Kealakekua Bay, a white obelisk commemorates the death of British Captain James Cook in 1779. In an accumulation of misunderstandings, Cook was killed. His expedition established the first contact between Hawai'i and the West, and would lead to irrevocable change.

Far Right: Kealakekua Bay, a designated state historical and underwater park, teems with marine life and colorful fish. The bay is a favorite spot for snorkelers and divers.

KOHALA

Defined by the volcanic Kohala Mountain, Kohala, on the Big Island's northwestern peninsula, forms the Big Island's oldest surface land. It opens to deep, eroded valleys with plunging waterfalls, and preserves memories of the island's rich cultural and historical past. Its sun-splashed white-sand beaches are the perfect setting for splendid golf courses and resorts.

Lapakahi, an ancient settlement, whispers of old fishing villages and secluded beach coves. On grassy coastal plains endure the stone walls of ancient Moʻokini Heiau, reconstructed in the 1300s, when the foreign priest Pāʻao established a new line of chiefs.

Kohala is the place where King Kamehameha was born and reared, some time around 1758. Eventually, a memorial statue would gaze down over Kohala's small towns. The annual King Kamehameha Day, June 11, is a celebration rich with ceremony, dance, and floral parades.

On Kohala's rolling slopes, where wild cattle once roamed, ranchers settled in. Among them was John Palmer Parker, who, in 1847, founded Parker Ranch. Spanish cowboys taught Hawaiian men skills with horses, lariats and ropes. Rodeos celebrate this paniolo heritage.

Sugar came to Kohala as elsewhere and left in its wake shuttered plantation stores. Narrow, inaccessible trails dug to build sugar ditches have slowly returned to the wilderness. Now, visitors come to Kohala to explore its varied past. Hiking and mule-riding adventures, kayak experiences, and artists' galleries in former plantation stores reveal Kohala's diversity.

Above: In windward Kohala, tropical flowers such as this dangling heliconia thrive.

Right: Mules graze pasture lands bordering Pololū Valley, at the end of Highway 270 in windward Kohala. Deep valleys and steep, verdant cliffs define the coastline in this oldest part of the Big Island, heavily eroded by weather and waves.

Grafted onto lava fields and hugging the Pacific Ocean, championship golf courses sprawl along the Kohala Coast. The Mauna Kea Beach Resort Golf Course, shown here at Hole Three, was designed by Robert Trent Jones Sr.

Right, inset: Legendary pro golfer and golf course designer Jack Nicklaus evaluates the next maneuver with his caddy, his son, at the Frances H. I'i Brown Golf Course at the Mauna Lani Resort.

Above: Award-winning chef Willy Pirngruber from the Hilton Waikoloa Village Resort poses with Waimea rancher Rick Habein on Waimea pasture lands. Kohala's farms and restaurants collaborate closely to create a fresh, regional cuisine.

Right: The Kohala Coast is famous for its splendid sunsets. The fabled green flash is often followed by a palette of pink, saffron, and ocher hues.

Above: Longboard surfers and their 9-foot-plus boards celebrate the creation of a Cultural Surf Park at Kawaihae Harbor in Kohala. Surfers gather here annually for the Pua Ka'ilimi Longboard Surfing Classic.

Left: In 1791, King Kamehameha I completed his massive temple, Pu'ukoholā Heiau, with walls that were twenty-feet thick. An oracle had said that its construction would ensure the chief's rulership over the islands. By 1810, the kingdom was indeed unified. The heiau is part of a national park.

Above: Guitar maker and musician David Gomes, born and reared in North Kohala, at home in his shop.

Left: Slack key guitarist, legendary storyteller, and falsetto singer Clyde "Kindy" Sproat was reared in Kohala's valleys. His art perpetuates the district's Hawaiian and paniolo heritage.

Far left, inset: Beloved in Kohala are Hawai'i Senator Daniel Akaka and his son Danny "Kaniela" Akaka Jr., who works as a cultural adviser in the area. The Akakas are known for their dedication to Hawai'i.

Left, background: Kohala Mountain, about 5,500-feet high, surfaced at least 600,000 years ago and is the Big Island's oldest land. Here, rolling green pastures slope down to the sea, rainfall is ideal for farming, and sunshine offers mesmerizing views.

Above: North Kohala is the birthplace of Kamehameha I, who united the islands under one rule in 1810. Each year, on June 11—King Kamehameha Day—the king's legacy is honored with ceremonies that start at dawn. The king's statue in Kapaʻau is carefully draped with leis.

Right: Young dancers in ti-leaf skirts wade into the sea in Kohala.

The scenic Kohala Mountain Road, Highway 250, meanders through 25-plus miles of ranching lands to connect the peninsula of North Kohala to the town of Waimea, home of Parker Ranch.

Left: On the plains south of Hāwī, the ruins remain of Moʻokini Heiau, first built in the fifth century. In the 1300s, the temple became the island's center of power, when the priest Pāʻao established a new line of chiefs. King Kamehameha I was born nearby, between 1753 and 1758.

All Photos: Each year, on July 4, the Parker Ranch Rodeo celebrates the area's paniolo (cowboy) heritage with riding and roping contests that draw the best cowboys in the state. Even keiki (children) participate in the competitions.

Background: Kohala's ranching days date back to the early 1800s, when herds of cattle roamed wild. Parker Ranch was founded in 1847 by John Palmer Parker, the first man to shoot cattle for the king. At Parker Ranch, the legendary Hawaiian cowboy, the paniolo, rose to national fame.

Above: Far removed from city lights and pollution, and seldom obscured by clouds, skies along the Kohala Coast offer exquisite opportunities for astronomers. Here, stargazers at 'Anaeho'omalu Bay.

Left: The arrival of Captain James Cook's vessels in January 1779 marked the onset of dramatic changes for the Hawaiian people. In this photo, a duplicate of Cook's boats sails along the Kohala Coast, which, within just two centuries, would become the site of ultramodern resorts.

HĀMĀKUA

Rainfall is plentiful and volcanic soils are old in the district of Hāmākua, north of Hilo, on the eastern, windward slopes of Mauna Kea and Kohala. Agriculture defines this gulch-rich area.

Its famous Waipiʻo Valley reaches six miles inland and is the largest valley in the state. Waterfalls plunge from near-perpendicular cliffs. In ancient times, chiefs and commoners were drawn to Waipiʻo's broad river plains, where the taro root thrived. Today, Waipiʻo farmers perpetuate the taro traditions.

Undeveloped, difficult to access, Waipiʻo is the symbol of a more tranquil Hawaiʻi, before westerners came. True, modern surfers venture down to ride the waves, but they cross the river by horse or foot, like before.

Sugar ruled most of Hāmākua from the late 1800s until the early 1990s, when its sole remaining mill closed. The highway traverses numerous sugar towns, which await new inspiration and capital. A transformation is already happening on Hāmākua's fallow sugar lands. Thanks to visionary chefs who are dedicated to local produce, farmers are experimenting with new and diversified crops.

The sacred summit of Mauna Kea falls within the Hāmākua District. Here, astronomers study the stars, extreme adventurers challenge the snow, and environmentalists protect a rare alpine ecosystem. More than anything, the summit is a sacred Hawaiian site, for Mauna Kea connects the Big Island in all its diversity to its one and only source: the universe.

Right: Gulches cross windward Hāmākua's former sugarcane lands to drain the district's frequent rains. Small towns along the coast saw their heyday during sugar plantation times.

Above: Taro root was the staff of life in ancient Hawaiian days: Waipiʻo, one of the most fertile valleys in the islands, once sheltered a major farming settlement. Taro pond fields continue to thrive on Waipiʻoʻs broad valley floor, where Wailoa river runs throughout the year.

Left: From the plantation town of ʻŌʻōkala through Honokaʻa, and to Waipiʻo, the Hāmākua coast runs about fifty miles in length. Just decades ago, when Hāmākua produced thousands of tons of sugar, its numerous plantation towns thrived.

In the early 1900s, during the heyday of sugar, cane fields defined the Hāmākua Coast. But in the decades following World War II, even the most advanced cost-saving techniques could not create a profit for the sugar industry. In 1993, Hāmākua's last remaining sugar company closed. Today, the cane fields are slowly shifting to a diversity of agricultural crops.

Surfboards in Hawai'i may have adapted to modern times, and horseback riding is more of a pastime than a necessity these days, yet the ways of Waipi'o have not changed. This unspoiled, river-rich valley is best traveled by foot or horse.

Above: The 1,600-foot Hiʻilawe Falls in the back of Waipiʻo Valley are the highest on the Big Island and are at the source of legends and myths. They plunge uninterrupted for at least 1,000 feet.

Left: Surrounded by sheer, nearly-perpendicular cliffs, young surfers stand on Waipiʻo's black-sand shores to contemplate the waves at dawn. Although difficult to reach, Waipiʻo is a favorite surfing spot for island residents.

Right: Hāmākua's scenic roads lead through gulches rich with flowering tropical trees.

Far Right: Along the rough Hāmākua Coast, waterfalls plunge into the ocean from steep and inaccessible cliffs.

Above: At the mouth of Waipi'o's Wailoa River, keiki play.

Left: From the late 1300s until around 1600, Waipi'o was home to the island's most powerful chiefs. Remains of at least six temples have been found. In 1779, Captain Cook estimated that about 2,500 people made the valley their home. Preserving their heritage, Hawaiian families continue to grow taro in Waipi'o valley. They now live an isolated farming life.

Since the installation of a first observatory in 1970, the 13,796-foot summit of Mauna Kea has emerged as the world's leading astronomical site. Today, thirteen telescope facilities staffed by experts from eleven countries probe the summit's clear, dry skies.

In winter months, the summit of Mauna Kea, "White Mountain" in the Hawaiian language, may be buried under a thick mantle of snow. Conditions are arctic, with high winds and intense ultraviolet light. Snowboarding enthusiasts do not mind.

Majestic Mauna Kea, the highest peak in the Pacific, is foremost
a sacred Hawaiian site, home to the snow goddess Poliʻahu, a place
for prayer and contemplation, where earth and sky connect.